BOOK ON SPACE:
ASTEROIDS AND METEORS

SPEEDY
PUBLISHING

Speedy Publishing LLC

40 E. Main St. #1156

Newark, DE 19711

www.speedypublishing.com

Every day, Earth is
bombarded with more
than 100 tons of dust
and sand-sized particles.

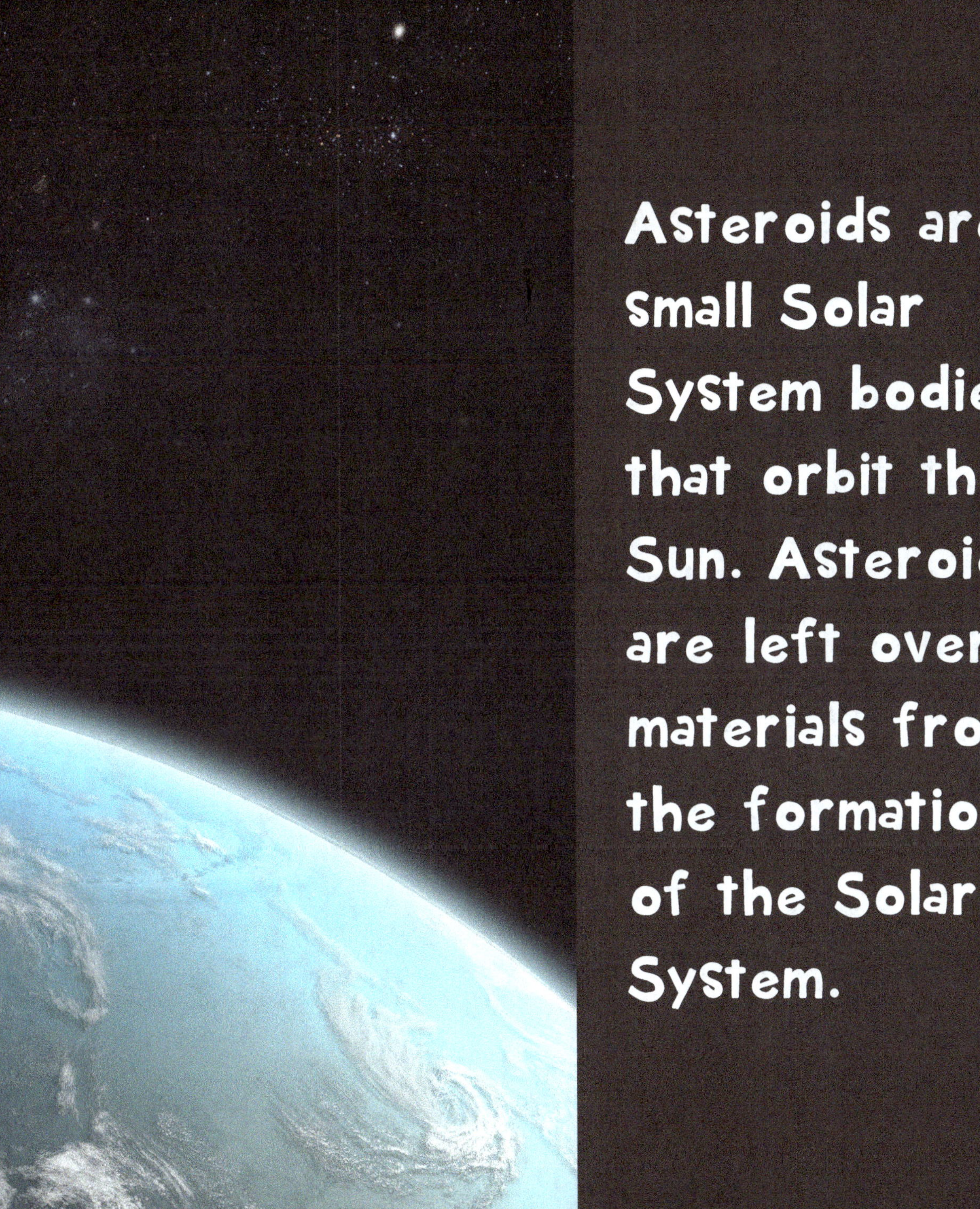

Asteroids are small Solar System bodies that orbit the Sun. Asteroids are left over materials from the formation of the Solar System.

Asteroids vary greatly in size, some feature diameters as small as ten metres while others stretch out over hundreds of kilometres.

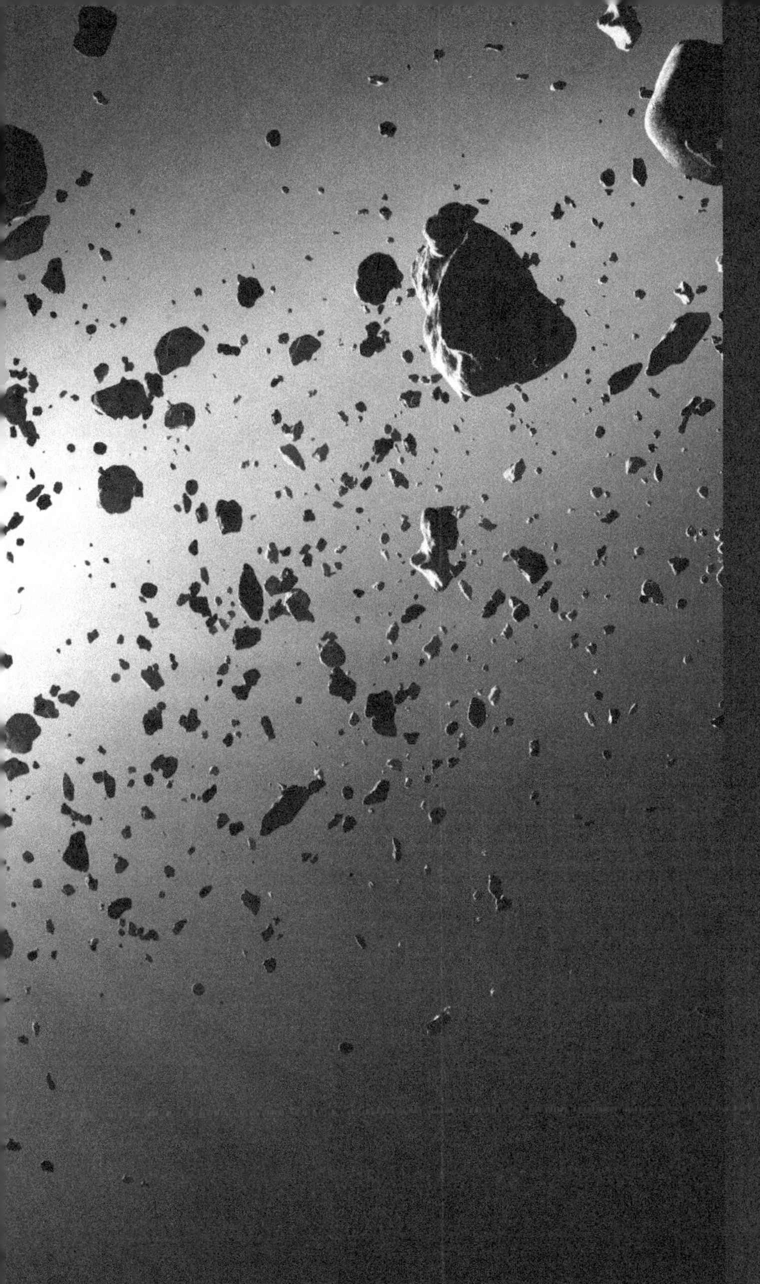

The large majority of known asteroids orbit in the asteroid belt between the orbits of Mars and Jupiter.

Asteroids are
rich in precious
metals and
other metals, as
well as water.

A meteoroid
that burns up
as it passes
through
the Earth's
atmosphere
is known as
a meteor.

Millions of
meteors occur
in the Earth's
atmosphere
daily. Most
meteoroids that
cause meteors
are about the
size of a grain
of sand.

Meteors can travel as slow as 25,000 mph and reach speeds up to 160,000 miles per hour.

* 9 7 9 8 8 6 9 4 4 9 8 4 9 *